THE SCIENCE OF **SUPERPOWERS**

THE SCIENCE OF
TIME TRAVEL

Peg Robinson

Cavendish
Square

New York

Published in 2019 by Cavendish Square Publishing, LLC
243 5th Avenue, Suite 136, New York, NY 10016

Website: cavendishsq.com

This publication represents the opinions and views of the author based on his or her personal experience, knowledge, and research. The information in this book serves as a general guide only. The author and publisher have used their best efforts in preparing this book and disclaim liability rising directly or indirectly from the use and application of this book.

All websites were available and accurate when this book was sent to press.

Library of Congress Cataloging-in-Publication Data

Author: Robinson, Peg.
Title: The science of time travel / Peg Robinson.
Description: New York : Cavendish Square, 2019. | Series: The science of superpowers | Includes glossary and index.
Identifiers: ISBN 9781502638021 (pbk.) | ISBN 9781502638038 (library bound) | ISBN 9781502638045 (ebook)
Subjects: LCSH: Time travel--Juvenile literature. | Physics--Juvenile literature. | Space and time--Juvenile literature.
Classification: LCC QB209.5 R63 2019 | DDC 530.11--dc23

Editorial Director: David McNamara
Editor: Kristen Susienka
Copy Editor: Rebecca Rohan
Associate Art Director: Amy Greenan
Designer: Joe Parenteau
Production Coordinator: Karol Szymczuk
Photo Research: J8 Media

The photographs in this book are used by permission and through the courtesy of: Cover AndreyL/Shutterstock.com; p. 4 (and hroughout book) Keith Pomakis/Wikimedia Commons/File:Cumulus Clouds Over Jamaica.jpg/CC BY SA 2.5; p. 4 lassedesignen/ Shutterstock.com; p. 6 Olga_Gavrilova/iStock; p. 7 Everett – Art/Shutterstock.com; p. 9 RGR Collection/Alamy Stock Photo; p. 10 Ann Ronan Pictures/Print Collector/Getty Images; p. 12 The Advertising Archives/Alamy Stock Photo; p. 14 Benjamin Shearn/ Stockbyte/Getty Images; p. 16 VasjaKoman/DigitalVision Vectors/Getty Images; p. 18 Lambert/Keystone/Hulton Archive/Getty Images; p. 21 JSC/NASA; p. 23 Everett Collection/ Alamy Stock Photo; p. 24 Jessie Eastland/Wikimedia Commons/File:Integratron-3. jpg/CC BY-SA 4.0; p. 27 Oto Godfrey and Justin Morton/Wikimedia Commons/ File:TeamTimeCar.com-BTTF DeLorean Time Machine-OtoGodfrey.com-JMortonPhoto. com-07.jpg/CC BY-SA 4.0; p. 31 Mark McClare/Shutterstock.com; p. 33 Ink Drop/Alamy Stock Photo; p. 34 DEA/G. NIMATALLAH/De Agostini Picture Library/Getty Images; p. 37 Tomas Sereda/iStock/Thinkstock; p. 38 Fabrice Coffrini/AFP/Getty Images; p. 41 Jurik Peter/Shutterstock.com; p. 42 Walter Myers/Stocktrek Images/Getty Images.

Printed in the United States of America

CONTENTS

CHAPTER 1

A HISTORY OF TIME TRAVEL

Time travel is one of the coolest superpowers. In stories, some superheroes use time travel to solve crimes. Others use it to rewrite history. In reality, time travel has excited scientists for many decades. People have spent a lot of time trying to figure out if humans can ever go back into the past or forward into the future. After all, who wouldn't like to travel in

Opposite: Time is a unique and essential part of our daily lives.

The Prague astronomical clock in the Czech Republic has been documenting the passage of time since the 1400s.

time? There are many ideas, called **theories**, out there about how we could time travel. However, are any of them true?

TIME TRAVEL IN STORIES

Many people have dreamed of traveling in time. Time traveling is talked about in **myths** and fairy tales from ancient cultures and in more recent eras. Some religious folktales also mention it. The usual kind of time travel found in religious traditions, legends, and folk and fairy tales involves time passing differently in two different worlds. These worlds are sometimes called **dimensions**. Such stories discussing this kind of time travel can be found in religions like Hinduism and Buddhism. Fairy tales from Japan, England, and other parts of the world also use this idea.

In this kind of story, a fairy or genie or some other **supernatural** being usually takes a human from the human world into a supernatural world.

This image of the legend of Rip Van Winkle was painted by John Quidor in 1849.

The human will stay there for what seems like a few hours or days. When they come back, they find that many years have passed. Time is faster or slower in the human world. In some stories, time is very fast. In others, the human comes back after what seems like a long time to find almost no time has gone by at all.

This idea is used in many modern stories and books. One of the most famous is *The Lion, the Witch and the Wardrobe* by C. S. Lewis. In this book, four children go to a different world, called Narnia, and stay there for many years. When they come back to their own world, no one even noticed they were gone—in their world, only a minute or so had passed. Other stories include "Rip Van Winkle," by Washington Irving, and the religious folktale "The Seven Sleepers of Ephesus." In "The Seven

This picture shows the main characters in the *Chronicles of Narnia* movie entering Narnia for the first time.

Ancient Time

Before clocks and watches were invented, it was hard to imagine traveling in time. Time was something that happened to you. Time meant growing old. Time meant the seasons passing. But people could not

Chronos

see time, hear time, or taste time. However, ancient cultures did have a sense of time. For example, the Greeks had Aeon. Aeon was a god of time. The Romans had Chronos. He was also a god of time. The Buddhists and Hindus believed that time passed differently in different spiritual realms. They developed a theory very similar to modern scientific theories of other worlds, or dimensions, to explain it.

Other cultures did measure the passage of time. The Chinese, the Aztecs, the Maya, the Persians, and others became experts at using the stars to measure time. Still, no stories of traveling through time like superheroes come from ancient cultures. That changed in the Victorian period, though, when clocks became popular. Suddenly, clocks and watches became easy to own. Everyone could learn how to tell the time. They could also imagine what it would be like to go back in time.

Sleepers," seven boys hide in a cave. They are trying to escape people who want to attack them. The boys hide in the cave for what they think is a little time. When they leave the cave, they discover that two hundred years have gone by!

MODERN TIME TRAVEL

The idea of being able to travel back and forth in time, on purpose, is very modern. The first stories began in the 1800s—over two hundred years ago. That may seem like a long time, but it's hardly any time at all compared to how long humans have been on Earth telling stories.

The English author Charles Dickens was one of the first modern people to write about traveling back and forth in time. His story, "A Christmas Carol," talks about a grouchy old **miser** named Ebenezer Scrooge. Scrooge is visited by ghosts (or spirits) of Christmas Past, Christmas Present, and Christmas Future. Each spirit takes Ebenezer Scrooge to different times and scenes in his past, his present, and his years to come. They teach him the importance of life and family.

Another author named H.G. Wells was the first person to tell a story about a machine that

H.G. Wells's *Time Machine* inspired other people to think of traveling to the past in a vehicle.

could travel in time. His 1895 novel *The Time Machine* is still popular today.

Once people began to write about time travel more often, it became a very popular power to explore in stories and books. Over the years, other authors and artists imagined what it would be like to have characters who could travel in time. Because of H.G. Wells, people think of things like time machines when they hear the words "time travel." Some popular characters in the twentieth and twenty-first centuries that can time travel include Hermione Granger in the Harry Potter series and the time-traveling Doctor Who.

SCIENCE AND TIME TRAVEL

Scientists have also imagined traveling in time. One of the people who thought about time travel was Albert Einstein. He lived in the twentieth century and made new theories about time travel. Two of his most well-known theories are called the theory of special relativity and the theory of general relativity.

The theory of special relativity states that nothing can travel faster than the speed of light. The speed of light is 186,000 miles per second (about 300,000,000 meters per second). The theory also describes an important kind of time called **space-time**. Space-time means that space and time are linked rather than being separate ideas.

In the theory of general relativity, space-time is changed by forces like gravity and light. Another idea, called time dilation, is that in time travel, you can move forward by going very fast or by escaping your planet's gravity.

None of these theories prove time traveling as we know it is possible, though.

CHAPTER 2

CAN WE TRAVEL IN TIME?

Is time travel really possible? Could anyone have it as a superpower? Or at least own a machine that could do the job? The answers to these questions have been explored for many years. In some instances, time traveling is possible. There is a normal way of time traveling and the way we think of time traveling.

Opposite: Some people imagine what it would be like to go back to the time of the dinosaurs.

THE WORKINGS OF TIME TRAVEL

What's the normal way? You're doing it right now. Yes—you, personally, sitting or standing or reading in bed. No matter who you are or what you're doing, *you* are a time traveler. Now. This very minute. Time is passing by quickly. The seconds are slipping away and soon are gone. In reality, we travel in time every day, in one direction: into the future. From when we wake up until we go to sleep, we are moving through time. We "time travel" at a rate of one hour per hour.

This image shows the ages of man, time traveling in the normal way.

So, one kind of time travel is possible, but not the way we imagine it. That leaves the question: Is the way we imagine time travel possible? Sort of. In order for time travel to happen, in theory, you have to have one of two things: very fast speed or a lot of gravity. These elements actually change the rate of time. On Earth, we have gravity, but we don't have the ability to travel faster than the speed of light. Other objects, like airplanes, do travel quickly, but not quickly enough to make time travel happen as we think it should.

DID YOU KNOW?

The idea of a **black hole** was first thought of in 1783 by an Englishman named John Michell. He called it a "dark star."

TIME IN SPACE

Many theories about time travel mention space. That is because in space, you have objects that pull in a lot of gravity and objects that travel very fast. There are also different rules in space.

Scientists like to explore the possibility of time travel in space. For example, some of Albert Einstein's theories talk about space-time.

Scientist Stephen Hawking also has thoughts about time traveling to other universes through black holes and **wormholes**.

Black holes are caused when a star collapses on itself. They have a lot of gravity. In fact, they have so much gravity that they can trap light, the fastest speed in the universe. According to

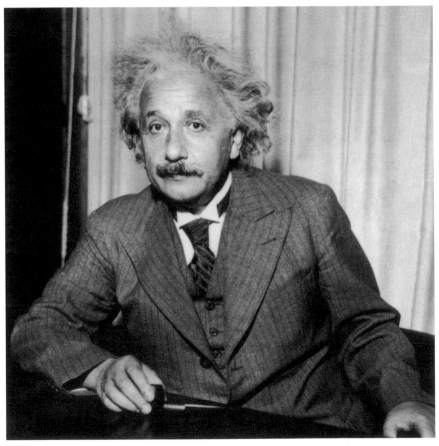

Albert Einstein's studies reveal a lot about time travel. Here he is in 1933.

Albert Einstein, nothing can travel faster than light. Some mathematicians and scientists think a black hole's gravity could be so strong that it could allow **particles** to go backward in time. Stephen Hawking has said that if there is a large black hole with a lot of gravity and **rotation**, it might be possible to go through a black hole into a different universe. However, it would be very difficult to ever come back. Dr. Hawking does not think we can ever travel to the past.

Wormholes have been dreamed about as time-traveling objects for decades. Wormholes are shortcuts through the universe that could let people travel through time. Writers and moviemakers have imagined sending spaceships through wormholes to go to other parts of the universe or into other universes or back into the past. However, some scientists think wormholes would collapse if you tried to use them for time travel.

THE FATE OF TIME TRAVEL

This is what most scientists think: the way we see time travel in movies, books, and comics is not possible. We can only move in one direction in time—into the future. A long trip, traveling away

A Real Time Traveler

There is someone who has experienced a scientific form of time travel. In fact, many astronauts have experienced it. The person who has spent the most time in space is Russian cosmonaut Sergei Krikalev. By 2013, he had spent almost 804 days living in the International Space Station. For all of that time he was outside of Earth's **gravity well**. Being outside a gravity well means time slows down for the person. Not by much—but by a tiny bit.

After many trips, totaling 803 days, 9 hours, and 39 minutes on the Space Station, Krikalev was two hundredths of a second behind Earth time. That's 0.02 seconds. When he came back to the planet, he traveled 0.02 seconds in time to "catch up" and rejoin Earth's time. That means he was traveling to the future.

Sergei Krikalev poses for a photo on the space shuttle *Discovery* in 2001.

from gravity wells very fast, would let you lose enough time to come back to Earth in "the future." But you'd have to spend a long time in space first, or travel much, much faster than scientists think the universe will let you go. Even so, people still hope one day time traveling might be possible.

THE PHILADELPHIA EXPERIMENT

While there are no working machines or technology to "travel in time," there are plenty of people who want to believe it's been done. One of the most famous legends of modern time travel is called the Philadelphia Experiment. The story is that during World War II, the United States government got many of the best scientists of the time to invent a device that made warships invisible. They tried, and it almost worked, but there were many side effects. One side effect was time travel.

The Philadelphia Experiment is not true history. It is a **hoax**. That means it's a tempting lie people tell to fool you about something in science or in history—or both. It is not true, but it's interesting. And many people enjoy the story just because it's so much fun.

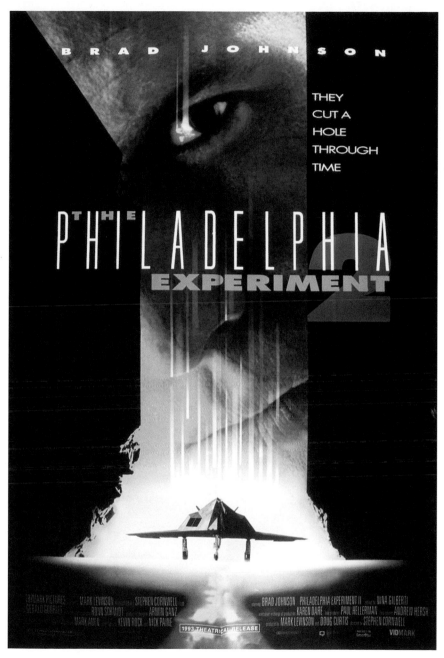

The Philadelphia Experiment legend became a movie in 1984 and 1993. This poster advertises the 1993 movie.

CHAPTER 3

TIME MACHINES, EQUATIONS, AND FROZEN FUTURES

While the kind of time traveling we see in movies and TV shows or read about in books might not be possible on Earth, that has not stopped

Opposite: George Van Tassel's Integratron "time machine" still exists today.

people from trying to create time machines or prove it is possible. Throughout history, there have been many people who have tried to understand the workings of time travel and reach into the future or see the past.

MODERN TIME TRAVELERS

Books and stories have made people think of time traveling machines differently. In the 1985 movie *Back to the Future*, the characters use a DeLorean sports car to travel to the past and return to the present. Other popular "time machines" in movies, TV shows, and comics include telephone booths, police boxes, and even a treadmill.

Some people think traveling to the past is impossible, while others think it could happen one day. Two such people are Ben Tippett and Ron Mallett. Both men have proposed that you can create time machines using strong forces, such as light, to bend time in a circle. This loop would allow people to travel back and forth in time. They could go to other parts of the universe and other dimensions. Ron Mallett has spent most of his life developing a mathematical equation for time traveling. He is also building a time machine that

In *Back to the Future*, the characters time travel in a DeLorean car.

he hopes will allow people to travel through time one day. However, many people believe he is wrong and his time machine and equation are impossible. Ben Tippett, a mathematician, has also tried to prove with math that time traveling is possible. However, Tippett does not think it will ever happen in our universe. Mallett thinks it could happen but with more advanced technology and more money put into projects like his.

Historically, others have tried to create time machines, but not in the way that we think of them today. In the 1940s and 1950s, many stories of Unidentified Flying Objects (UFOs) and aliens began to appear in the United States. One person who became involved with this trend was a man named George Van Tassel. George Van Tassel told a story about how an alien life form visited him one night. The alien told him to go to the desert and build. Listening to the alien's words, Van Tassel set out to build a building in 1953. It would become a time machine. The time machine he wanted to create wouldn't take you to the future or to the past though. It was a time machine that would restore your body to look and feel younger. It would make you live longer. The time machine was called Integratron. It was built in Landers, California. It was a round building made without metal or screws. Some people believed his time machine would work. Others thought Van Tassel was creating a hoax.

Van Tassel died before the building was completed. Soon after, the machines in the building that would make the time machine work were removed. No one knows where they went. However, the building was bought by two sisters in 2000, was finished, and remains in its chosen spot today. It is used as a place of healing, meditation, and music recording.

EXPERIMENTS WITH TIME TRAVELING

While the Philadelphia Experiment is one of the most well-known stories about experimenting with time travel, others exist. One story is called the Montauk Project. Although rumors existed for decades, this story gained popularity in 1982. That year, Preston Nichols published the book *The Montauk Project: Experiments in Time*. This book documented Nichols's and others' supposed experiences in a US government project at Camp Hero. Camp Hero was part of an Air Force station

Back from Time?

Many people, including scientists, would like to find some answer to time travel. Why? Because sometimes it would be nice to be able to go forward without aging. What if you could go to sleep for decades or centuries and wake up all that time later looking and feeling no older than you were when you went to sleep?

There is real hope we could do that. The science behind this idea is called "cryonics." It could let us time travel into the future.

Right now, it's mostly science fiction. Companies are looking into it though. Cryonics involves taking someone and freezing them. Years later, someone would unfreeze them and revive them in a future world. No one knows yet if we can put people to sleep for years without aging, or freeze them and then bring them back. But we know people can enter comas and come back from them. We also know that humans can be injured or can drown in very deep cold and instead of killing them, the cold preserves them. So there is hope that some day we could apply these ideas to have cryonic time travel.

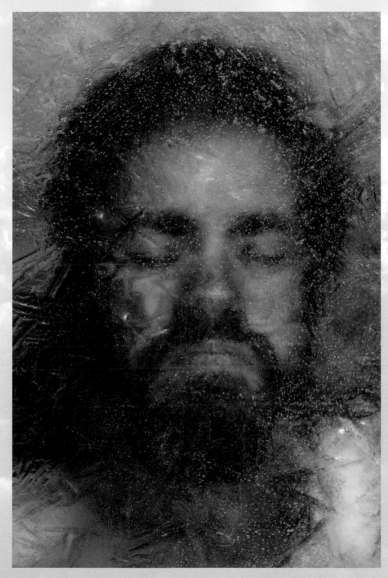

This image shows a man frozen in ice. Maybe freezing people will be a way of time traveling to the future.

An English girl, who is only known as "JS," went to court before dying of cancer. She demanded the right to be frozen. She hoped that someday a way would be found to wake her up and cure her cancer. She won her case. In 2016, she was cryogenically frozen by a company in the United States after she died.

in Montauk, Long Island, New York. Nichols stated the US government had been doing top-secret experiments on children. These experiments dealt with time travel, mind control, telepathy, and monsters. Later, it inspired the hit TV show *Stranger Things*.

Another experiment with time travel was done in 2015. This experiment involved light particles. In the experiment, light particles seemed to travel at faster-than-light speeds and actually seemed to travel backward in time. However, this was a **phenomenon** called time reversal. It was demonstrated through the use of high-speed cameras.

TV shows like *Stranger Things* use legends like the Montauk Project in their storylines.

CHAPTER 4

SCIENCE, TIME TRAVEL, AND THE UNKNOWN

T ime traveling may be explored in science fiction for a while. However, modern scientists are trying to test Einstein's theories of relativity and possibly discover ways to travel into the future.

Opposite: Sir Isaac Newton, who developed three laws of motion

NEWTON AND PHYSICS

To develop working time travel, we would have to learn new and surprising things about a science called physics. Physics is the study of happenings around us, like gravity. During the past century or so, experiments have led to major shifts in our understanding of physics.

Before the early 1900s, the main type of physics was Newtonian physics. It was developed by Sir Isaac Newton in the late 1600s and early 1700s.

Newton was a great scientist. His work in physics and calculus let people understand how things move better than ever before. Almost everything people care about in ordinary life can be described using Newtonian physics.

EINSTEIN AND SPECIAL PHYSICS

In the early 1900s, Albert Einstein and other scientists worked out "special" laws of physics. Their work opened up unexpected possibilities. Because of this new understanding, nuclear bombs, nuclear power plants, and new forms of medicine all became possible. New ideas can change what we think is possible.

Today, physics helps us understand how nuclear power works.

During almost the same period, other scientists like Max Planck, Niels Bohr, and Werner Heisenberg developed what is called quantum physics. Quantum physics studies the behavior of super-small particles. These particles are called subatomic particles. They behave in very weird ways. They are so weird that Albert Einstein used the word "spooky" to describe them.

Quantum physics does not work like the physics Newton and Einstein developed. We do not know why. Einstein's science made new things possible. If we work out how quantum physics and Newtonian physics can both be true, we could find ways to make time travel work. It is not likely, but it leaves room for surprises.

STUDYING SURPRISES

Today, the main experiments that might change how we understand time travel have to do with quantum physics. One exciting place where quantum physics is being explored today is the Large Hadron Collider. Based in Switzerland, this is a large tube deep underground. Inside the tube particles move very fast and collide with each other. These collisions let scientists develop new ideas about how physics works.

The Large Hadron Collider is so big people bicycle around it.

The Large Hadron Collider is the largest machine in the world. Experiments there explore many different things. Some try to find a way to travel faster

DID YOU KNOW?

Did you know that time is the only dimension in which you can only move one way?

than the speed of light. If that is possible, then there is a chance time traveling could happen. Other experiments test time travel directly. They try to show particles moving in time.

The Large Hadron Collider lets scientists copy how particles might behave in wormholes or in black holes. Remember, these are two places that scientists think time travel might be possible.

Scientists think they might be able to create and study tiny black holes safely. If so, we could learn how subatomic particles behave near black holes and try to understand why they behave that way.

ALTERNATE DIMENSIONS

Alternate dimensions are realities existing "next door" to our universe. Science thinks that all possible worlds exist. These worlds are layered beside each other. Like time travel, not many think we could ever go there—except in fun stories or movies. But if we could, there are people who hope different dimensions might let us go to the future, exactly the same way as in old stories. By stepping outside our own world, it would be like visiting Narnia or some other fantasy world, or being one of the Seven Sleepers. We could come back from a slower dimension into the future.

TESTING WORMHOLES

Some scientists are trying to observe wormholes. Remember, wormholes are tunnels, or shortcuts, in the universe. They connect one part of space-time with another part. Scientists think wormholes may exist when the conditions are just right. Some think that means something very exceptional happens. This could be something like a star exploding. Others think there have to be special materials called "exotic matter" for wormholes to form.

Some scientists think that wormholes would let subatomic particles go backward in time. This is because if they exist, a wormhole would make a tunnel in space-time. The tunnel would have two ends. Each end would be in a different space and could be in a different time. A subatomic particle traveling through the wormhole could move forward or backward in time.

This is one artist's concept of what a wormhole could look like.

Right now scientists do not think that kind of time travel is possible for humans though. They're not even sure it would work for subatomic particles. And they're not sure how a person could reach and experiment with a wormhole safely.

If scientists' ideas about wormholes are right, then they will try to work out what to do with time-traveling particles. They will also keep looking for ways to make more things have superpowers.

For now, it seems time traveling the way we think about it will continue to be fictional. However, maybe one day quantum physics will tell us something that could make time traveling possible.

Studying Space

One of the best ways to study space and the happenings within our universe is through the use of telescopes. In January 2017, the space agency NASA announced it would send three space telescopes into space to measure characteristics of different space objects. One of the objects is a black hole. The telescopes will be launched in 2020. They will measure an object's radiation and other qualities. They will not actually be able to see the object up close. The telescopes will gather measurement information and send it back to scientists on Earth. The scientists will then use the information to answer some questions about black holes and other space objects. It could help scientists better understand different, unique, and interesting objects in space.

This image imagines what NASA's Chandra X-ray Observatory telescope might look like thousands of miles from Earth.

GLOSSARY

BLACK HOLE A large object in space that sucks in a lot of gravity.

DIMENSIONS Other worlds in the universe that could be traveled to through wormholes or other time-traveling methods.

GRAVITY WELL The amount of gravity a large object, such as a planet or a black hole, has.

HOAX A lie set up to look true.

MISER A person who is greedy and hoards money, who won't share or spend money normally.

MYTHS Stories from ancient cultures.

PARTICLE Units of matter and energy, including protons, neutrons, and electrons, that are smaller than atoms.

PHENOMENON A special event.

ROTATION Spinning motion.

SPACE-TIME A word used to describe the reality formed within space and time together.

SUPERNATURAL Anyone or anything that seems to be outside, beyond, or above the normal laws of reality.

THEORY An idea that is meant to be tested and proved right or wrong.

WORMHOLE A tunnel, or shortcut, between one place in space-time to another place.

FIND OUT MORE

BOOKS

Bell, Jim. *The Space Book: From the Beginning to the End of Time*. New York: Sterling, 2013.

Perlov, Delia, and Alex Vilenkin. *Cosmology for the Curious*. New York: Springer, 2017.

Pickover, Clifford A. *The Physics Book: From the Big Bang to Quantum Resurrection*. New York: Sterling, 2011.

Pohlen, Jerome. *Albert Einstein and Relativity for Kids: His Life and Ideas with 21 Activities and Experiments*. Chicago, IL: Chicago Review Press, 2012.

WEBSITES

Business Insider: Two Types of Time Travel
http://www.businessinsider.com/how-to-time
-travel-with-wormholes-2017-11

On this website, watch Professor Brian Greene from Columbia University discuss two types of time travel: into the past and into the future.

Kinooze: What Is Time?
http://kinooze.com/what-is-time

Visit this website to learn more about time and how other cultures told time or recorded time.

NASA SpacePlace: Is Time Travel Possible?
https://spaceplace.nasa.gov/dr-marc-space/en/#/
review/dr-marc-space/time-travel.html

This website explores whether time travel could happen.

INDEX

Page numbers in **boldface** are illustrations. Entries in **boldface** are glossary terms.

ABOUT THE AUTHOR

Peg Robinson is a writer and editor. She graduated from the University of California at Santa Barbara, with honors, and attended Pacifica Graduate Institution. She served for two years as a docent for Opus Archives, focusing on converting historically significant audio recordings to digital format, securing valuable material in a less fragile recording medium. She lives in Rhode Island with her daughter and her cat and dog.